THE RIME OF
THE ANCIENT MARINER

Samuel Taylor Coleridge (1772–1834), one of the most imaginative poets of the English Romantic Movement, was also its most influential thinker and philosopher. *The Rime of the Ancient Mariner* was written early in his life, during a period of intense and impassioned creativity, and, like all his best work, has a visionary quality with strong religious and metaphysical overtones.

Mervyn Peake (1911–1968) was born in China but moved to England at the age of eleven and studied at Eltham College, Kent, and at the Royal Academy Schools. His striking originality as an artist brought him renown as an illustrator of books such as *Alice in Wonderland*, *The Hunting of the Snark* and *Treasure Island*. He also wrote poetry and plays, but is best remembered as a writer for his Gormenghast trilogy of novels, *Titus Groan*, *Gormenghast* and *Titus Alone*, an extravagant gothic fantasy which has become a modern classic.

Samuel Taylor Coleridge

THE RIME OF THE ANCIENT MARINER

ILLUSTRATED BY
Mervyn Peake

WITH AN INTRODUCTION BY
Marina Warner

V

VINTAGE

Published by Vintage 2004

2 4 6 8 10 9 7 5 3 1

First published in Great Britain in 1949 by
Chatto & Windus

Vintage
Random House, 20 Vauxhall Bridge Road,
London SW1V 2SA

Random House Australia (Pty) Limited
20 Alfred Street, Milsons Point, Sydney
New South Wales 2061, Australia

Random House New Zealand Limited
18 Poland Road, Glenfield,
Auckland 10, New Zealand

Random House (Pty) Limited
Endulini, 5A Jubilee Road, Parktown 2193,
South Africa

The Random House Group Limited Reg. No. 954009
www.randomhouse.co.uk

A CIP catalogue record for this book
is available from the British Library

ISBN 0 09 944499 2

Papers used by Random House are natural, recyclable
products made from wood grown in sustainable forests.
The manufacturing processes conform to the environ-
mental regulations of the country of origin

Printed and bound in Great Britain by
Cox & Wyman Ltd, Reading, Berkshire

INTRODUCTION

The Rime of the Ancient Mariner recounts spells and charms, fits and trances, and, like 'Kubla Khan' and 'Christabel', which Coleridge also wrote during the same amazing year (1797–8), the poem enacts the spellbinding it describes. While reading the *Rime* or listening to it on tape, we become the mesmerised Wedding Guest; like him we are drawn into the story almost against our will, commanded to follow the flaring and leaping of Coleridge's images as hallucinatory phantoms rise one after the other, and enigma follows enigma. The deliberate, faux-naif simplicity of the ballad metre gives the poem a rocking pulse that forbids halting at any stanza; the internal rhymes pull from line to line inexorably while the end-stopped rhymes add touches of stiff, jagged syncopation.

In a kind of mimetic music, the scheme reproduces the fevered, fitful movement of the Mariner's ship, now skimming swiftly along, now swerving back, now driven suddenly this way and that. Coleridge catches his readers up into the Mariner's uncanny odyssey as he sails into the icescapes of the South Pole and then round the Horn, and speeds northwards in the Pacific towards the scorching doldrums near the Equator (though it isn't in fact possible to chart the exact course of the ship). Like Jane Eyre's mind-voyaging in her youth, through enraptured gazing at engravings of remote regions and exotic fauna and flora, Coleridge's compulsive story unfolds a marine geography of terrible extremes and fabulous wonders: looming icebergs, the gigantic Albatross, and the peculiar horror of such a phenomenon as:

> Yea, slimy things did crawl with legs
> Upon the slimy sea.

The scenery catches the moods of the magic lantern shows, the Phantasmagoria which were beginning to be shown as public entertainment in that decade, with their appropriate stage effects, as when the sea, 'like a witch's oils, / Burnt green, and blue, and white.'

This hallucinatory vividness and pace obscure what is actually happening – or rather, they are so deeply intertissued into the very nature of the story Coleridge tells that the details of what occurs become less important (this is also true of 'Kubla Khan' and 'Christabel' – the plots' rationales remain mysteries and their meanings remain elusive). Not surprisingly, the poem began with a dream, told by a neighbour to Wordsworth who then passed it on to Coleridge. At first, the two poets intended to collaborate, as on some other poems, but their approaches to the uncanny material diverged strongly, and Wordsworth fell away. Subsequently he harshly criticised the *Rime's* 'supernatural machinery' and Coleridge cut many lines from the more lurid Gothic passages for the second edition of *Lyrical Ballads* in 1800.

The original fragment Wordsworth communicated included the death of the Albatross and the dominant motifs of accursedness and wandering. The Mariner was a figure of Cain, a criminal and an outcast. As J.C.C. Mays, one of the editors of the *Collected Works*, has commented, Coleridge returned to the poem repeatedly, putting it through several different versions, for the *Rime* 'became a mirror in which Coleridge came to see his fate as endlessly reflected.'[1]

The Mariner commits sacrilege, killing the Albatross that was following the ship. At first the bird's appearance gives him and the other sailors great joy, and so it is never clear why he lifts his cross-bow and shoots it. As William Empson has commented, it was probably obvious to anyone at the time that he killed the bird for food: any sea story reveals how sailors long for something other than a diet of dry biscuits.[2] But Coleridge omits to tell us this – or even suggest it – and this hole where a motive might be opens the poem's involving mediation on fated wrongdoing, on existential despair, on folly and unconscious acts. Coleridge communicates his anguish about nature and divine creation, in which the noble solitary bird has its place along with slimy things: the Mariner, in shooting the bird, transgresses against the harmonious wholeness of creation, and the vitality that must be respected in every living thing. As the Mariner tells the Wedding Guest towards the very end:

> He prayeth best, who loveth best
> All things both great and small;
> For the dear God who loveth us,
> He made and loveth all.

When he's able to see this wholeness in creation, the curse on the Mariner is lifted: the penance he has to perform is worked out only after he is able to see the beauty of the world without prejudice or hostility. He has come to admire the watersnakes, and their 'rich attire', their every track 'a flash of golden fire'. In this state of grace, he comes to regain that happy child-like vision described by Coleridge in 'The Aeolian Harp':

> Methinks, it should have been impossible
> Not to love all things in a world so fill'd...

When the *Rime* was criticised by his contemporaries like Mrs. Barbauld, for not having a moral, Coleridge was aggrieved, for he felt that if anything, by the standards of lyrical expressiveness, the poem puts its message across too didactically.

During this inspired period of poetic writing, Coleridge was fretting about his Christian faith, having trouble with the problem of evil, and *The Rime of the Ancient Mariner* encloses a vision of the supernatural that veers strongly towards a mystical Gnosticism and away from his own Unitarianism. This vision involves angels, spirits and spectres battling for the souls of men – including the Mariner's – and a complicated, spooky struggle between life and death. In the marginal glosses which Coleridge began adding to the poem in 1800, and published with all subsequent versions until the edition of 1817, he gives references to sources in classical and Neoplatonist philosophy.[3] But the poem stubbornly refuses explication at the level of discursive thinking, and its contra-puntal accompaniment serves less to clarify what the dramatic conflict involves than to reveal Coleridge's own perplexity. Characteristically, his thought shifts to and fro between Imag-ination and Understanding. The *Rime* ventriloquises the Mariner, but it also uses the two storytelling voices – in verse and in prose – one enthralled, even entranced by the unfolding drama that propels the action forward, while the other, from the margins, comments in a contemplative mood, couched in metaphysical imagery, on the incidents as they unfold. He amplifies the Mariner's lonely prayer for homecoming in Part Four, for example, with a mini excursus of haunting beauty about the journeys of the stars to 'their appointed rest'.

But the glosses lay on another stratum of bafflement, in my view, one that deepens the dark and pain in the poem, casts its matter as a form of possession, and throws into relief its deep resistance to rational elucidation.

For the *Rime* is rightly considered a supreme artefact of imagination, an extended and dazzling product of nightmare, of the state of mind that Coleridge described to his friend Thomas Poole the month before he started writing the poem:

> Frequently have I (half-awake and half-asleep, my body diseased and fevered by my imagination) seen armies of ugly things bursting in upon me, and these four angels (by his bed) keeping them off.[4]

What circumstances contributed to the curse Coleridge describes? His own complex nature, the volatility in his personal relations, his difficulties with work and survival, his disturbed health and drug-taking – all these elements certainly added to the potent charm he was stirring in the cauldron of his imagination. But the contemporary political struggles that lay foremost in Coleridge's concerns at the time affect his poem's stricken protagonist and his story, and they can be glimpsed, I believe, beneath the phantasmagoric cascade of images.

Bristol was a hub of the three-corned traffic, and from its wharves manufactured goods were shipped to the West Coast of Africa in exchange for slaves; these were then transported to the West Indies; the sugar grown on the plantations where the slaves were put to work was then carried back to Bristol and other ports. And so the cycle was completed, only to start up again. In 1795, Coleridge gave a passionate lecture in Bristol, 'On the Slave Trade', which became the basis of an essay published the year before he wrote the *Rime*. At the same time, he translated part of his 'Ode on the Slave Trade' from Greek for inclusion in Southey's epic poem *Joan of Arc*. (He had written it for a prize at Cambridge in 1792 while still an undergraduate.)[5] In a city deeply entangled in this traffic and enriched by its profits, he painted ferocious pictures of the cruelties suffered by the slaves, and he also imagined the flight of their spirits back to their native lands, rather like the stars journeying to their appointed rest: he knew enough African eschatology to communicate this soul-travel after death into another part of this world, rather than to another, otherworldly realm.

In other poems at this time, Coleridge was exploring states of fantasy through writing about beliefs held by different peoples and the effects of outward experiences on inward consciousness. But from the point of view of *The Rime of the Ancient Mariner*, it is above all significant that Coleridge's attack on slavery focuses on guilt by association. Responsibility gnaws him, and underpins one of his most anguished calls for an end to the traffic: not only for the slaves but for all of you, he cries, who are standing by, like himself, while it goes on. He passes from invoking the hideous torments of the victims, which he declares surpass even Dante's hellish imaginings, to the horrors of the effects on all who are engaged in the traffic, but also those who stand at a distance and reap the profits:

> And is it not an allowed axiom in morality, that wickedness may be multiplied, but cannot be divided; and that the guilt of all, attaches to each one who is knowingly an accomplice? Think not of the slave-captains and slaveholders! These very men, their darkened minds, and brutalized hearts, will prove one part of the dreadful charge *against you*!' (emphasis added)[6]

In the *Rime's* phantasmic and accursed voyage, Coleridge transfigured the imperial enterprise and its cost to all its participants: slavers, slaves and unwitting associates. As William Empson wrote, the poem is 'the great ballad of maritime expansion and empire'.[7]

The political context presents a possible interpretation of the psychology in the poem and its influences. In his reading far and wide, Coleridge had come across accounts of soul theft and spell-binding performed by communities in the Caribbean and in North America, and he acknowledges the influence of their ideas about magic healings and afflictions, about the power of curses and charms, multiple souls, wandering spirits and the living dead, or the zombie. Entrancement is one of Coleridge's most obsessive motifs; all three of his great feverish visions, 'Kubla Khan', 'Christabel' and *The Rime of the Ancient Mariner* feature overpowered individuals, enchained by some supernatural or uncanny force. The poems' protagonists exist in an in-between state, neither dead nor alive, driven by something outside themselves that has 'o'ermastered' them. After the death of the Albatross, the Mariner says, 'I thought that I had died in sleep, / And was a blessed ghost.' The doomed ship moves, bewitched, laden with its 'ghastly crew', all of them living dead whose sounds and terrible, accursed looks deepen the narrator's enchanted state. When the other ship, a 'naked hulk', a 'spectre-bark' of skeletal rig, draws alongside, the Night-mare Life-in-Death appears on it, throwing dice with Death himself. Life-in-Death wins the Mariner, the gloss tells us, and so he escapes death:

> a thousand thousand slimy things,
> Lived on; and so did I.

The ship becomes a ghost ship, the Mariner a stricken, enthralled automaton, and while the sea rots, the dead men do not, but still have eyes that continue to curse him:

> The cold sweat melted from their limbs,
> Nor rot nor reek did they:
> The look with which they looked on me
> Had never passed away.

Daemons mysteriously descend to revivify the crew's 'corses', and work the sails. Several more episodes, mostly remaining enigmatic and unresolved in meaning, permutate the concept of the living dead. Interestingly, some of Coleridge's changes for the second edition deliberately erased the African or American Gothic effects in favour of pagan Gnostic imagery closer to home, and with these revisions, some of the original zombie-like character of the curse on the Mariner and on the ship weakened. Coleridge added, for example, that the agents of the crew's resurrection were specifically 'a troop of spirits blest', and he cut the stanza describing the dead men raising their right hands, ablaze, while:

> Their stony eye-balls glitter'd on
> In the red and smoky light.

He also cut the following stanza:

> Then vanish'd all the lovely lights;
> The bodies rose anew:
> With silent pace, each to his place,
> Came back the ghastly crew.

Literally revenants, the 'ghastly crew' anticipates the zombies in later horror films such as the 1969 classic *The Night of the Living Dead*.

Mental enchantment is a psychological state, wrought by human rather than divine powers to take control of another and bind the victim; sometimes, as in Coleridge's poems and, soon after, in Keats' analogous studies in enchantment, 'Lamia' and 'La Belle Dame sans Merci', the inward mind moves in unholy union with the charms cast upon it – 'witchery by daylight'. Coleridge's anxiety about outside circumstances and other men's acts doing him personal harm, and even bewitching him into a compulsive life-in-death, performs an interesting step sideways from the issue of slavery's principal victims. The zombie ultimately is no longer body on whom the magical operation is performed, instead the zombie becomes the person who performs the deed, in this case the Mariner. This inversion happens again and again in magical plot structures about the power of the oppressed to attack their oppressors with witchcraft: the original subjugated character of the living-dead slips out of register with its prime subject, the economic human chattel, and turns into a susceptible and stricken member of the masters' class who is to blame as well. The Ancient Mariner, won by Life-in-Death and doomed to wander, with whom Coleridge identified so strongly, may well be the first English zombie.[8]

*   *   *

The vividness of the images in *The Rime of the Ancient Mariner* has inspired many artists – Gustave Doré with his 1878 illustrations setting a very high standard of intense imagination. Mervyn Peake began his sequence in 1942, while he was suffering from the mental trouble that dogged him all his life. He'd been invalided out of the army and wrote from Southport Emergency Hospital to his publisher, Harold Raymond at Chatto and Windus, describing with some wit and little self-pity the routine designed to cure his 'neurosis'. Raymond immediately replied suggesting Peake illustrate Coleridge's great ballad. The powerful sequence of engravings that resulted from this inspired invitation shows the influence of Peake's French predecessor in the nervy hatching and stippling, the telescoped and attenuated figures and plunging vistas. Mervin Peake's use of deep blacks, welling shadows and horrible phantoms captures shudderingly the Gothic atmosphere of Coleridge's poem. But his most horribly beguiling illustration of all shows Coleridge's 'Night-mare Life-in-Death' as a noseless death's-head vamp, with a blonde mane and lipsticked mouth and kittenish crossed skeleton hands. She proved too strong meat for the times and Chatto and Windus quietly dropped her from the first 1943 edition, Raymond writing that he found 'the leprous lady' too terrifying. Peake published her elsewhere, but she had to wait till 1973 to be reunited with the poem.[9]

Mervyn Peake patterns the page with dramatic economy, and his Ancient Mariner looms out in the first illustration, a gaunt and prophetic 'greybeard loon' gesturing with his long skinny hands and fixing us, in the place of the Wedding Guest, with his uncanny gig-lamp eyes, while in the final image we see only the back of the spellbound Mariner as he walks on, a revenant looking for more victims, evoking with perfect reticence and mystery the lines that might stand so well as Coleridge's own epitaph:

> I pass, like night, from land to land;
> I have strange power of speech.

Marina Warner
2003

NOTES

1. Samuel Taylor Coleridge *Collected Works: Poems (Reading Texts)*, Part 1, ed. J.C.C. Mays (Princeton, 2001), pp. 336 ff.
2. William Empson.
3. Taken from Marsilio Ficino's translation of *Neoplatonists*, which Coleridge asked Thelwall to buy for him, in 1796.
4. Letter to Poole, Oct 9 1797, from Samuel Taylor Coleridge *A Selection of His Poems and Prose*, ed. Kathleen Raine (London, 1957), p.117.
5. Anthea Morrison, 'Samuel Taylor Coleridge's Greek Prize "Ode on the Slave trade"', from *An Infinite Complexity: Essays in Romanticism*, ed. J.R. Watson (Edinburgh 1983), pp. 145-160: 145.
6. 'On the Slave Trade', *Collected Works of STC The Watchman*, Vol 2, ed Lewis Patton, (London, 1970) pp. 130-140.
7. Empson, op. cit.
8. For more detail on zombies and Coleridge's interest, see Marina Warner, *Fantastic Metamorphoses, Other Worlds: Ways of Telling the Self* (Oxford, 2001). pp. 119-160.
9. G. Peter Winnington, *Vast Alchemies: The Life and Work of Mervyn Peake* (London, 2000) pp. 155-8, 159-65.

THE RIME OF
THE ANCIENT MARINER

PART ONE

IT is an ancient Mariner,
And he stoppeth one of three.
"By thy long grey beard and glittering eye,
Now wherefore stopp'st thou me?

The Bridegroom's doors are opened wide,
And I am next of kin;
The guests are met, the feast is set:
May'st hear the merry din."

He holds him with his skinny hand,
"There was a ship," quoth he.
"Hold off! unhand me, grey-beard loon!"
Eftsoons his hand dropt he.

He holds him with his glittering eye—
The Wedding-Guest stood still,
And listens like a three years' child:
The Mariner hath his will.

The Wedding-Guest sat on a stone:
He cannot choose but hear;
And thus spake on that ancient man,
The bright-eyed Mariner.

"The ship was cheered, the harbour cleared,
Merrily did we drop
Below the kirk, below the hill,
Below the light-house top.

The Mariner
tells how the ship
sailed southward
with a good
wind and fair
weather, till it
reached the Line.

The sun came up upon the left,
Out of the sea came he!
And he shone bright, and on the right
Went down into the sea.

Higher and higher every day,
Till over the mast at noon—"
The Wedding-Guest here beat his breast,
For he heard the loud bassoon.

The Wedding-
Guest heareth
the bridal music;
but the Mariner
continueth his
tale.

The bride hath paced into the hall,
Red as a rose is she;
Nodding their heads before her goes
The merry minstrelsy.

The Wedding-Guest he beat his breast,
Yet he cannot choose but hear;
And thus spake on that ancient man,
The bright-eyed Mariner.

The ship
driven by a storm
toward the South
Pole.

"And now the Storm-blast came, and he
Was tyrannous and strong:
He struck with his o'ertaking wings,
And chased us south along.

With sloping masts and dipping prow,
As who pursued with yell and blow
Still treads the shadow of his foe,
And forward bends his head,
The ship drove fast, loud roared the blast,
And southward aye we fled.

And now there came both mist and snow,
And it grew wondrous cold:
And ice, mast-high, came floating by,
As green as emerald.

The land of ice, and of fearful sounds, where no living thing was to be seen.

And through the drifts the snowy clifts
Did send a dismal sheen:
Nor shapes of men nor beasts we ken—
The ice was all between.

The ice was here, the ice was there,
The ice was all around:
It cracked and growled, and roared and howled,
Like noises in a swound!

Till a great sea-bird, called the Albatross, came through the snow-fog, and was received with great joy and hospitality.

At length did cross an Albatross,
Thorough the fog it came;
As if it had been a Christian soul,
We hailed it in God's name.

It ate the food it ne'er had eat,
And round and round it flew.
The ice did split with a thunder-fit;
The helmsman steered us through!

And lo! the Albatross proveth a bird of good omen, and followeth the ship as it returned northward through fog and floating ice.

And a good south wind sprung up behind;
The Albatross did follow,
And every day, for food or play,
Came to the mariners' hollo!

In mist or cloud, on mast or shroud,
It perched for vespers nine;
Whiles all the night, through fog-smoke white,
Glimmered the white moon-shine."

The ancient Mariner inhospitably killeth the pious bird of good omen.

"God save thee, ancient Mariner!
From the fiends, that plague thee thus!—
Why look'st thou so?"—"With my cross-bow
I shot the Albatross."

4

PART TWO

"The Sun now rose upon the right:
Out of the sea came he,
Still hid in mist, and on the left
Went down into the sea.

And the good south wind still blew behind,
But no sweet bird did follow,
Nor any day for food or play
Came to the mariners' hollo!

*His shipmates
cry out against
the ancient
Mariner, for
killing the bird of
good luck.*

And I had done a hellish thing,
And it would work 'em woe:
For all averred, I had killed the bird
That made the breeze to blow.
Ah wretch! said they, the bird to slay,
That made the breeze to blow!

*But when the
fog cleared off,
they justify the
same, and thus
make themselves
accomplices in the
crime.*

Nor dim nor red, like God's own head,
The glorious Sun uprist:
Then all averred, I had killed the bird
That brought the fog and mist.
'Twas right, said they, such birds to slay,
That bring the fog and mist.

*The fair breeze
continues; the
ship enters the
Pacific Ocean,
and sails north-
ward, even till it
reaches the Line.
The ship hath
been suddenly
becalmed.*

The fair breeze blew, the white foam flew,
The furrow followed free;
We were the first that ever burst
Into that silent sea.

Down dropt the breeze, the sails dropt down,
'Twas sad as sad could be;

And we did speak only to break
The silence of the sea!

All in a hot and copper sky,
The bloody Sun, at noon,
Right up above the mast did stand,
No bigger than the Moon.

Day after day, day after day,
We stuck, nor breath nor motion;
As idle as a painted ship
Upon a painted ocean.

Water, water, every where,
And all the boards did shrink;
Water, water, every where
Nor any drop to drink.

*And the
Albatross begins
to be avenged.*

The very deep did rot: O Christ!
That ever this should be!
Yea, slimy things did crawl with legs
Upon the slimy sea.

About, about, in reel and rout
The death-fires danced at night;
The water, like a witch's oils,
Burnt green, and blue, and white.

And some in dreams assured were
Of the Spirit that plagued us so;
Nine fathom deep he had followed us
From the land of mist and snow.

*A Spirit had
followed them;
one of the
invisible in-
habitants of this
planet, neither
departed souls nor*

*angels; concerning whom the learned Jew, Josephus, and the Platonic Constantinopolitan,
Michael Psellus, may be consulted. They are very numerous, and there is no climate or
element without one or more.*

7

And every tongue, through utter drought,
Was withered at the root;
We could not speak, no more than if
We had been choked with soot.

Ah! well-a-day! what evil looks
Had I from old and young!
Instead of the cross, the Albatross
About my neck was hung."

PART THREE

"THERE passed a weary time. Each throat
Was parched, and glazed each eye.
A weary time! a weary time!
How glazed each weary eye,
When looking westward, I beheld
A something in the sky.

The ancient Mariner beholdeth a sign in the element afar off.

At first it seemed a little speck,
And then it seemed a mist;
It moved and moved, and took at last
A certain shape, I wist.

A speck, a mist, a shape, I wist!
And still it neared and neared:
As if it dodged a water-sprite,
It plunged and tacked and veered.

At its nearer approach, it seemeth him to be a ship; and at a dear ransom he freeth his speech from the bonds of thirst.

With throats unslaked, with black lips baked,
We could nor laugh nor wail;
Through utter drought all dumb we stood!
I bit my arm, I sucked the blood,
And cried, A sail! a sail!

A flash of joy:

With throats unslaked, with black lips baked,
Agape they heard me call:
Gramercy! they for joy did grin,
And all at once their breath drew in,
As they were drinking all.

And horror follows. For can it be a ship that comes onward without wind or tide?

See! see! (I cried) she tacks no more!
Hither to work us weal;

Without a breeze, without a tide,
She steadies with upright keel!

The western wave was all a-flame.
The day was well nigh done!
Almost upon the western wave
Rested the broad bright Sun;
When that strange shape drove suddenly
Betwixt us and the Sun.

And straight the Sun was flecked with bars,
(Heaven's Mother send us grace!)
As if through a dungeon-grate he peered
With broad and burning face.

It seemeth him but the skeleton of a ship.

Alas! (thought I, and my heart beat loud)
How fast she nears and nears!
Are those her sails that glance in the Sun,
Like restless gossameres?

Are those her ribs through which the Sun
Did peer, as through a grate?
And is that Woman all her crew?
Is that a Death? and are there two?
Is Death that woman's mate?

And its ribs are seen as bars on the face of the setting Sun. The Spectre-Woman and her Death-mate, and no other on board the skeleton-ship. Like vessel, like crew!

Her lips were red, her looks were free,
Her locks were yellow as gold:
Her skin was as white as leprosy,
The Night-mare Life-in-Death was she,
Who thicks man's blood with cold.

The naked hulk alongside came,
And the twain were casting dice;
'The game is done! I've won! I've won!'
Quoth she, and whistles thrice.

Death and Life-in-Death have diced for the ship's crew, and she (the latter) winneth the ancient Mariner.

11

The Sun's rim dips; the stars rush out:
At one stride comes the dark;
With far-heard whisper, o'er the sea,
Off shot the spectre-bark.

No twilight within the courts of the Sun.

We listened and looked sideways up!
Fear at my heart, as at a cup,
My life-blood seemed to sip!
The stars were dim, and thick the night,
The steersman's face by his lamp gleamed white;
From the sails the dew did drip—
Till clomb above the eastern bar
The horned Moon, with one bright star
Within the nether tip.

At the rising of the Moon,

One after one, by the star-dogged Moon,
Too quick for groan or sigh,
Each turned his face with a ghastly pang,
And cursed me with his eye.

One after another,

Four times fifty living men,
(And I heard nor sigh nor groan)
With heavy thump, a lifeless lump,
They dropped down one by one.

His shipmates drop down dead.

The souls did from their bodies fly,—
They fled to bliss or woe!
And every soul, it passed me by,
Like the whizz of my cross-bow!"

But Life-in-Death begins her work on the ancient Mariner.

PART FOUR

"I FEAR thee, ancient Mariner!
I fear thy skinny hand!
And thou art long, and lank, and brown,
As is the ribbed sea-sand.

The Wedding-Guest feareth that a Spirit is talking to him.

I fear thee and thy glittering eye,
And thy skinny hand, so brown."—
"Fear not, fear not, thou Wedding-Guest!
This body dropt not down.

But the ancient Mariner as-sureth him of his bodily life, and proceedeth to re-late his horrible penance.

Alone, alone, all, all alone,
Alone on a wide, wide sea!
And never a saint took pity on
My soul in agony.

He despiseth the creatures of the calm.

The many men, so beautiful!
And they all dead did lie:
And a thousand thousand slimy things
Lived on; and so did I.

And envieth that they should live, and so many lie dead.

I looked upon the rotting sea,
And drew my eyes away;
I looked upon the rotting deck,
And there the dead men lay.

I looked to Heaven, and tried to pray;
But or ever a prayer had gusht,
A wicked whisper came, and made
My heart as dry as dust.

I closed my lids, and kept them close,
And the balls like pulses beat;
For the sky and the sea, and the sea and the sky
Lay like a load on my weary eye,
And the dead were at my feet.

But the curse liveth for him in the eye of the dead men.

The cold sweat melted from their limbs,
Nor rot nor reek did they:
The look with which they looked on me
Had never passed away.

An orphan's curse would drag to hell
A spirit from on high;
But oh! more horrible than that
Is the curse in a dead man's eye!
Seven days, seven nights, I saw that curse,
And yet I could not die.

In his loneliness and fixedness he yearneth towards the journeying Moon, and the stars that still sojourn, yet still move onward; and every where the blue sky belongs to them, and is their appointed rest, and their native country and their own natural homes, which they enter unannounced, as lords that are certainly expected, and yet there is a silent joy at their arrival.

The moving Moon went up the sky,
And no where did abide:
Softly she was going up,
And a star or two beside.

Her beams bemocked the sultry main,
Like April hoar-frost spread;
But where the ship's huge shadow lay,
The charmed water burnt alway
A still and awful red.

By the light of the Moon he beholdeth God's creatures of the great calm.

Beyond the shadow of the ship,
I watched the water-snakes:
They moved in tracks of shining white,
And when they reared, the elfish light
Fell off in hoary flakes.

Within the shadow of the ship
I watched their rich attire:
Blue, glossy green, and velvet black,
They coiled and swam; and every track
Was a flash of golden fire.

O happy living things! no tongue
Their beauty might declare:
A spring of love gushed from my heart,
And I blessed them unaware:
Sure my kind saint took pity on me,
And I blessed them unaware.

*Their beauty and
their happiness.*

*He blesseth them
in his heart.*

The selfsame moment I could pray;
And from my neck so free
The Albatross fell off, and sank
Like lead into the sea."

*The spell begins
to break.*

17

PART FIVE

"Oh sleep! it is a gentle thing,
Beloved from pole to pole!
To Mary Queen the praise be given!
She sent the gentle sleep from Heaven,
That slid into my soul.

By grace of the holy Mother, the ancient Mariner is refreshed with rain.

The silly buckets on the deck,
That had so long remained,
I dreamt that they were filled with dew;
And when I awoke, it rained.

My lips were wet, my throat was cold,
My garments all were dank;
Sure I had drunken in my dreams,
And still my body drank.

I moved, and could not feel my limbs:
I was so light—almost
I thought that I had died in sleep,
And was a blessed ghost.

He heareth sounds and seeth strange sights and commotions in the sky and the element.

And soon I heard a roaring wind:
It did not come anear;
But with its sound it shook the sails,
That were so thin and sere.

The upper air burst into life!
And a hundred fire-flags sheen,
To and fro they were hurried about!
And to and fro, and in and out,
The wan stars danced between.

And the coming wind did roar more loud,
And the sails did sigh like sedge;
And the rain poured down from one black cloud;
The Moon was at its edge.

The thick black cloud was cleft, and still
The Moon was at its side:
Like waters shot from some high crag,
The lightning fell with never a jag,
A river steep and wide.

The loud wind never reached the ship,
Yet now the ship moved on!
Beneath the lightning and the Moon
The dead men gave a groan.

The bodies of the ship's crew are inspired, and the ship moves on;

They groaned, they stirred, they all uprose,
Nor spake, nor moved their eyes;
It had been strange, even in a dream,
To have seen those dead men rise.

The helmsman steered, the ship moved on;
Yet never a breeze up blew;
The mariners all 'gan work the ropes,
Where they were wont to do;
They raised their limbs like lifeless tools—
We were a ghastly crew.

The body of my brother's son
Stood by me, knee to knee:
The body and I pulled at one rope
But he said nought to me."

"I fear thee, ancient Mariner!"
"Be calm, thou Wedding-Guest!
'Twas not those souls that fled in pain,
Which to their corses came again,
But a troop of spirits blest:

*But not by the
souls of the men,
nor by dæmons of
earth or middle
air, but by a
blessed troop of
angelic spirits,
sent down by the
invocation of the
guardian saint.*

For when it dawned—they dropped their arms,
And clustered round the mast;
Sweet sounds rose slowly through their mouths,
And from their bodies passed.

Around, around, flew each sweet sound,
Then darted to the Sun;
Slowly the sounds came back again,
Now mixed, now one by one.

Sometimes a-dropping from the sky
I heard the sky-lark sing;
Sometimes all little birds that are,
How they seemed to fill the sea and air
With their sweet jargoning!

And now 'twas like all instruments,
Now like a lonely flute;
And now it is an angel's song,
That makes the heavens be mute.

It ceased; yet still the sails made on
A pleasant noise till noon,
A noise like of a hidden brook
In the leafy month of June,
That to the sleeping woods all night
Singeth a quiet tune.

Till noon we quietly sailed on,
Yet never a breeze did breathe:

Slowly and smoothly went the ship,
Moved onward from beneath.

Under the keel nine fathom deep,
From the land of mist and snow,
The spirit slid: and it was he
That made the ship to go.
The sails at noon left off their tune,
And the ship stood still also.

The Sun, right up above the mast,
Had fixed her to the ocean:
But in a minute she 'gan stir,
With a short uneasy motion—
Backwards and forwards half her length
With a short uneasy motion.

Then like a pawing horse let go,
She made a sudden bound:
It flung the blood into my head,
And I fell down in a swound.

How long in that same fit I lay,
I have not to declare;
But ere my living life returned,
I heard, and in my soul discerned
Two voices in the air.

'Is it he?' quoth one, 'Is this the man?
By Him who died on cross,
With his cruel bow he laid full low
The harmless Albatross.

The spirit who bideth by himself
In the land of mist and snow,

He loved the bird that loved the man
Who shot him with his bow.'

The other was a softer voice,
As soft as honey-dew:
Quoth he, 'The man hath penance done,
And penance more will do.' "

PART SIX

First Voice

" 'But tell me, tell me! speak again,
Thy soft response renewing—
What makes that ship drive on so fast?
What is the ocean doing?'

Second Voice

'Still as a slave before his lord,
The ocean hath no blast;
His great bright eye most silently
Up to the Moon is cast—

If he may know which way to go;
For she guides him smooth or grim.
See, brother, see! how graciously
She looketh down on him.'

First Voice

*The Mariner
hath been cast
into a trance; for
the angelic power
causeth the
vessel to drive
northward
faster than
human life
could endure.*

'But why drives on that ship so fast,
Without or wave or wind?'

Second Voice

'The air is cut away before,
And closes from behind.

Fly, brother, fly! more high, more high!
Or we shall be belated:
For slow and slow that ship will go,   •
When the Mariner's trance is abated.'

*The super-
natural motion is
retarded; the
Mariner
awakes, and his
penance begins
anew.*

I woke, and we were sailing on
As in a gentle weather:

24

'Twas night, calm night, the moon was high
The dead men stood together.

All stood together on the deck,
For a charnel-dungeon fitter:
All fixed on me their stony eyes,
That in the Moon did glitter.

The pang, the curse, with which they died,
Had never passed away:
I could not draw my eyes from theirs,
Nor turn them up to pray.

The curse is finally expiated.

And now this spell was snapt: once more
I viewed the ocean green,
And looked far forth, yet little saw
Of what had else been seen—

Like one, that on a lonesome road
Doth walk in fear and dread,
And having once turned round walks on,
And turns no more his head;
Because he knows a frightful fiend
Doth close behind him tread.

But soon there breathed a wind on me,
Nor sound nor motion made:
Its path was not upon the sea,
In ripple or in shade.

It raised my hair, it fanned my cheek
Like a meadow-gale of spring—
It mingled strangely with my fears,
Yet it felt like a welcoming.

Swiftly, swiftly flew the ship,
Yet she sailed softly too:
Sweetly, sweetly blew the breeze—
On me alone it blew.

Oh! dream of joy! is this indeed
The light-house top I see?
Is this the hill? is this the kirk?
Is this mine own countree?

*And the ancient
Mariner be-
holdeth his
native country.*

We drifted o'er the harbour-bar,
And I with sobs did pray—
O let me be awake, my God!
Or let me sleep alway.

The harbour-bay was clear as glass,
So smoothly it was strewn!
And on the bay the moonlight lay,
And the shadow of the Moon.

The rock shone bright, the kirk no less,
That stands above the rock:
The moonlight steeped in silentness
The steady weathercock.

And the bay was white with silent light
Till rising from the same,
Full many shapes, that shadows were,
In crimson colours came.

*The angelic
spirits leave the
dead bodies,*

A little distance from the prow
Those crimson shadows were:
I turned my eyes upon the deck—
Oh, Christ! what saw I there!

*And appear in
their own forms
of light.*

Each corse lay flat, lifeless and flat,
And, by the holy rood!
A man all light, a seraph-man,
On every corse there stood.

This seraph-band, each waved his hand:
It was a heavenly sight!
They stood as signals to the land,
Each one a lovely light;

This seraph-band, each waved his hand,
No voice did they impart—
No voice; but oh! the silence sank
Like music on my heart.

But soon I heard the dash of oars,
I heard the Pilot's cheer:
My head was turned perforce away,
And I saw a boat appear.

The Pilot and the Pilot's boy,
I heard them coming fast:
Dear Lord in Heaven! it was a joy
The dead men could not blast.

I saw a third—I heard his voice:
It is the Hermit good!
He singeth loud his godly hymns
That he maketh in the wood.
He'll shrieve my soul, he'll wash away
The Albatross's blood."

PART SEVEN

"This Hermit good lives in that wood
Which slopes down to the sea.
How loudly his sweet voice he rears!
He loves to talk with marineres
That come from a far countree.

He kneels at morn, and noon, and eve—
He hath a cushion plump:
It is the moss that wholly hides
The rotted old oak-stump.

The skiff-boat neared: I heard them talk,
'Why, this is strange, I trow!
Where are those lights so many and fair,
That signal made but now?'

'Strange, by my faith!' the Hermit said—
'And they answered not our cheer!
The planks looked warped! and see those sails,
How thin they are and sere!
I never saw aught like to them,
Unless perchance it were

Brown skeletons of leaves that lag
My forest-brook along;
When the ivy-tod is heavy with snow,
And the owlet whoops to the wolf below,
That eats the she-wolf's young.'

*The Hermit of
the Wood,*

*Approacheth the
ship with
wonder.*

'Dear Lord! it hath a fiendish look—
(The Pilot made reply)
I am a-feared'—'Push on, push on!'
Said the Hermit cheerily.

The boat came closer to the ship,
But I nor spake nor stirred;
The boat came close beneath the ship,
And straight a sound was heard.

The ship
suddenly sinketh.
Under the water it rumbled on,
Still louder and more dread:
It reached the ship, it split the bay;
The ship went down like lead.

The ancient
Mariner is
saved in the
Pilot's boat.
Stunned by that loud and dreadful sound,
Which sky and ocean smote,
Like one that hath been seven days drowned
My body lay afloat;
But swift as dreams, myself I found
Within the Pilot's boat.

Upon the whirl, where sank the ship,
The boat spun round and round;
And all was still, save that the hill
Was telling of the sound.

I moved my lips—the Pilot shrieked
And fell down in a fit;
The holy Hermit raised his eyes,
And prayed where he did sit.

I took the oars: the Pilot's boy,
Who now doth crazy go,
Laughed loud and long, and all the while
His eyes went to and fro.
'Ha! ha!' quoth he, 'full plain I see,
The Devil knows how to row.'

30

And now, all in my own countree,
I stood on the firm land!
The Hermit stepped forth from the boat,
And scarcely he could stand.

'O shrieve me, shrieve me, holy man!'
The Hermit crossed his brow.
'Say quick,' quoth he, 'I bid thee say—
What manner of man art thou?'

The ancient Mariner earnestly entreateth the Hermit to shrieve him; and the penance of life falls on him.

Forthwith this frame of mine was wrenched
With a woful agony,
Which forced me to begin my tale;
And then it left me free.

Since then, at an uncertain hour,
That agony returns:
And till my ghastly tale is told,
This heart within me burns.

And ever and anon throughout his future life an agony constraineth him to travel from land to land.

I pass, like night, from land to land;
I have strange power of speech;
That moment that his face I see,
I know the man that must hear me:
To him my tale I teach.

What loud uproar bursts from that door!
The wedding-guests are there:
But in the garden-bower the bride
And bride-maids singing are:
And hark the little vesper bell,
Which biddeth me to prayer!

O Wedding-Guest! this soul hath been
Alone on a wide, wide sea:

So lonely 'twas, that God himself
Scarce seemed there to be.

O sweeter than the marriage-feast,
'Tis sweeter far to me,
To walk together to the kirk,
With a goodly company!—

To walk together to the kirk,
And all together pray,
While each to his great Father bends,
Old men, and babes, and loving friends,
And youths and maidens gay!

And to teach, by his own example, love and reverence to all things that God made and loveth.

Farewell, farewell! but this I tell
To thee, thou Wedding-Guest!
He prayeth well, who loveth well
Both man and bird and beast.

He prayeth best, who loveth best
All things both great and small;
For the dear God who loveth us,
He made and loveth all."

The Mariner, whose eye is bright,
Whose beard with age is hoar,
Is gone: and now the Wedding-Guest
Turned from the bridegroom's door.

He went like one that hath been stunned,
And is of sense forlorn:
A sadder and a wiser man
He rose the morrow morn.